How a Wound Became a Garden

Kellie Kaminskas

How a Wound Became a Garden
Published by Clover Moon Publishing
Hamden, CT

Copyright ©2026 by Kellie Kaminskas. All rights reserved.
KellieKaminskas.com

Cover artwork by Ella Woodward
Cover design by Amanda Miller, amandamillerpublishing.com
Interior design by Asya Blue Design, asyablue.com
All design copyrights © Kellie Kaminskas

POETRY / General
ISBN: 979-8-218-82516-4 (paperback)
Also available in Ebook.

QUANTITY PURCHASES: Schools, companies, professional groups,
clubs, and other organizations may qualify for special terms when
ordering quantities of this title. For information, email kellie.
kaminskas@yahoo.com.

Printed in the United States of America.

DEDICATION

Dearest You,

I have spent my days
rooted in shade,
where the light never lingered long enough.
I was pressed deeper,
hidden from sight.
Yet, still I reached
stretching, clawing through earth,
trusting that somewhere
my light could rise,
and shine just as bright.
There were whispers,
serpents hissing at the edges,
dismissing my fate,
casting stones at the gifts
I was born to create.
So, I gathered the shadows,
and I gathered the light.
I wove every wound
into every nook,
not into a single poem,
but into a whole book.

PART ONE

Cultivation

Wolf eyes,
lies.
Poison,
his demise.
I'll learn,
to love myself
through the hurting.
Dwelled with the dragon,
for far too many seasons.
Never could give me a reason.
Spoons, cotton, rock, bones.
Screaming,
leave me the fuck alone!
Dreaming,
the promise of
a peaceful home.

I fight
in my sleep,
until my fingers bleed.
Lay my tear-soaked cheek,
against the cotton sheets.
This is not a want;
this is not a need.
I pound my chest,
silently scream.
Living nightmare,
haunted dreams.
Highs and lows,
extreme.
Peace unseen.
Heaven must be serene.
Promise me.
Cover up your tracks.
Blood droplets,
confetti the sleeves.
Rip it from the seams.
Don't you dare lie to me.
Paint the pretty picture,
for everyone to see.
You were a monster
underneath.

⌣⟶

Losing my mother,
eviscerated me.
Shredded the fibers
of my being.
Swallowed me whole with
one gulp.
Cancer dimmed her
cashmere grey eyes.
That pain,
engulfed me
like an angry wave at sea.
Drowned me.
Ripped my naive faith
In this world.
The bad
kind of pain.

Birthing my son,
reincarnated me.
I want to swim
in his deep brown eyes.
Eyes the same as mine.
His sweet skin,
still vaguely scented
with my milk.
My love for him,

a mother's sweet ache.
Fills the empty pocket
of where he once grew.
Stitched together the heart,
so carefully created.
The good kind of pain.

⌒

Buried in the ground.
I scream,
nothing comes out.
Encased with satin,
pine-scented box.
I dug this grave;
is it mine?
Who will come
to take my soul?
No heaven. No hell. Just this.
Twisted bliss.
Silence.
Deafening quiet.
Smell the fresh dirt,
hear the moving earth.
I clutch the blood-red roses,
ones they picked to match
my painted lips.
Count all my sins.
Is this where life ends,
or begins?

Eerie flashes
of scraping shovels,
as they sliced
through the earth.
Did my best

to let them know,
it was not my time to go.
The faint light of the sun
oozing through the cracks
of my skeleton home,
is fading away.
Night will be upon me soon,
coldness is setting in.
My body is growing numb;
the air
escaping my lungs.
Panic has replaced,
the laugh lines on my face.
Each breath is
shorter,
sharper.

I am falling under.
My mind is full
of rumbled thunder.
My lungs,
bursting.
Body yearning,
begging the earth
make me your own.

Paradise,
the devil's fiery throne.
Intoxicated,
the sweet smell of death.
Take.
Me.
Home.

I prayed tonight.
Although I believe,
there's no god in sight.
Down on my knees,
my ends frayed tonight.
I'll fight the fight,
pick up the pieces.
The corners of my mind,
are quiet.
Close my eyes,
colors vibrant.
Breathe in deeply,
hush the crying.
Sleep is rushed,
nonexistent.
Fix it.
Fix this.

Mama, what do the clouds taste like; does the air
feel the same?
Does the wind carry my whispers of quiet pain?
When I cry the salty kind of tears, does it rain?
Years have passed, nothing has been the same.
The darkness just grows deeper, finders keepers.
I feel lost in a midnight ocean, commotion.
Waves are covering me, pushing me out to sea.
Fight every breath.
Life has only brought death.
What is left, Mama? What is next?
I need the sunrises, not just the sunsets.

A screaming quiet,
heart versus mind,
riot.
I'd be lying,
if I called this
anything but
surviving.
Slumber
far from reach.
Whisper to the edge
walking sleep.
Silently creep,
toes touch the rocks
that roll down
into the steep.
Heartbeat,
weep,
repeat.

Immersed,
in devastation.
Shredded,
limb from limb.
I'll gladly die
for the sins.
The hot heat
blood-boiling
fire roaring within.
My hands are empty,
body cold.
Toe tag my soul.
Lock me in the secret drawer,
throw away the key.
Hand the torch over,
ignite the flames.
Hell won't ever
be the same.

I wish I didn't know things. I asked myself, what's it going to take to grow my wings? The taste of blood, the smell of rock; cooked. The ringing in my head, bruises overlooked. The feel of ribs cracked as I ran my hands over my bones.

Quiet Queen of a battered home. It's your fault, you should have known. Devil displaced from his throne. A wall of polished colored wood. Pick a color, then another. It's been only a year since I buried my mother. I wanted to leave my shoes, caked with winter mud around the hole they prepared for you. Black velvet boots taught me to run. The only thing I kept, buried in the closet. To remind myself he will never hurt me again.

The haunting makes its way to my dreams most nights. The fear, never flight; always fight. Cold sweats, the feel of fists upon your chest. Venomous spit drips down your neck. Close your eyes . . . is it over yet? Widow's web, safety net.

I want a red-line adventure
where history gets swept away
with the same brooms
that soared in the sky
for the enchantment
of another day.
Do certain places
call to you?
A cosmic pull.
A familiar memory,
all your own.
Maybe it's because
I walked the stones
with my mother.
It could be part
of her heavenly home.

Days that seem
forever ago.
When twenty felt pure,
untouched earth.
A blue yarn hat,
empathetic soul.
That store is not open,
anymore.
When October,
used to be cold.

A barren land
can offer plenty,
just as a shiny penny.
Reap what's been sewn,
quietly before the snow.
Be still,
as seasons
come and go.
Conceive the notion,
the world will
continue to grow.
It's out
of control.

We've been fed,
how the devil
was once an angel.
Punishment
for temptation.
I look better
in red.
Life is sweeter,
living deliciously
on the edge.
I'd light
the black flame,
sink my teeth
into the flesh
of forbidden fruit.

Quietly listening,
to the snake
spew venomous moods.
Dare me,
I spoke.
I fear the living,
not the dead.
For I have lived,
in the earthly

depths of hell.
I know it well.
In all of us,
the beast
can dwell.

I had wanted so badly to grow up. To rush away my
youth, to stop playing house. But the walls turned out
to be made of cards, where ghosts roam my halls, and
I want nothing more than to go back. When bodies
weren't broken, and the world wasn't hurting. So badly.
It's as if we've all just gone mad, and our mothers aren't
here anymore to kiss away the salty tears firing down
our cheeks. Time just passes week after week, spirits
weak. Most nights I stir around the witching hour,
closing my eyes to try to remember. The blue and white
tree house perched in the center of four trees that my
dad built for me. I colored the walls with sidewalk chalk,
dreaming of what life would be. By the devil's hour I
must force sleep, for the shadows know their keep.
No matter where I go, they memorize my street.
A hurricane tore down that tree house. I moved back
into my childhood home to raise my boy; I still look at
those trees on the nights I can't sleep.

Consume me.
My heavy darkness,
faint light.
Midnight,
my prime.
Do my eyes shine
in the night?
Trace the lines
of my palms.
I'm a storm,
amid calm.
Autumn rain-
scented dawn.

Sun tea. One of my earliest memories. In the heat of
the summer mornings, my mother would put out a glass
coffee carafe full of water, fresh lemons, and bags of
black tea as dark as the sea. She'd bring it in when the
sky was sunset pink, and the crickets sang. I swear the
whole yard would smell of it. My cup was full. She was
jean jackets, tortoise shell sunglasses, Elizabeth Arden
Sunflowers perfume, small gold hoop earrings, and
Trident gum.

Scorpio,
ready to go.
Sting you,
if I need to.
Suck the poison out,
you won't want to live
without
me.

Witchy woman.
Light the fire,
at my feet.
They're going to burn
all of us in a fleet.
Flames engulf me.
They feel so sweet,
when you don't surrender
to defeat.

Outsider,
born a fighter.
Never back down,
fire within me.
A lighter.
Survivor.
For so long
I was prisoner,
to a war that wasn't mine.
Tightrope,
walking the line.
Rip my limbs,
from the vines.
Heaven or hell?
Divine.

I will never be
sunshine.
I am a moonlit night.
Knobby knees,
Dot my i's
cross your t's.
An open book,
never a mystery.
Hungry wolf,
bare teeth.
Remove the sword,
from my sheath.
Survivor,
mama's fighter.

I think
you need her
more,
when you're older.
Your mother.
Your creator,
safe harbor.
Only you know,
her heartbeat
from the inside.
Once she floats on,
you don't hear it anymore.
The hollow hum,
falls quiet.
Life turns,
defiant.
Lose her,
lose yourself.
I need
my mother.

Woman.
Bones strong,
carrying the weight of it all.
Don't bend,
don't let them
see you fall.
You have no choice,
but to stand tall.
House of bricks,
steady walls.
Keep the wolf,
from wrecking the halls.
Endure.
Keep the allure.

Hide your flaws
with makeup,
a nip, a tuck.
Solemnly swear,
you don't give a fuck.
When you're down
on your luck,
who is picking you up?
Bust your ass,
to make less
of a buck.

Work.
Stay home.
Have babies,
have none.
Be a wife,
be independent.
Do it all.
Don't fail,
be number one.
An endless battle,
never won:
Woman.

Midlife crisis,
whisper your vices.
Midnight lifeless,
heart pumping
in the quiet.
The sky paints me,
dying stars.
The moon reflects
to tell me,
"I will stay,
where you are."
Sliver in the sky,
sad eyes.
Sweet heat,
the middle of June
salts my hair.
Wildflowers,
bloom.

When I was as little as could be, I remember dreaming of being a fairy in Fern Gully. I guess I haven't changed much, still finding solace in the canopy of trees. I like the forest best when the sky is storming, the rain cupped in leaves. It's the quietest then, people flee. I soak it in, like the dirt below. Rainfall like teardrops. Wash away, baptize me. I prefer to feel small amongst towering trees, with a heart so big beating inside me. I tuck myself away on the cliffs carved so gracefully into the earth. Value their worth. Breathe in the breeze dancing on the tops of trees, let the rain pour down on me. Wandering fairy chasing dreams.

They would've burned me too,
with the others accused.
The biggest thing to fear,
is an unwavering woman.
For I am not one,
to bite my tongue.
Upon my broom,
fly around the moon.
Illuminate the darkness,
when the blade is sharpest.
Scatter me amongst
the golden, fallen leaves.
For when the Earth weeps,
I will grow again
under brave feet.

I have lived in hell, burning.
Lips painted red like flames.
Yearning.
I've tasted the blood, curdling.
Screams.
I've placed my face on the lap of the beast,
begging him for peace.
With one hand on his bell, the other my cheek.
He rang a melodic feast.
The taste so sweet.
Life is delicious.

She was
skin and bones,
cold as stone.
Together,
but alone.
He chased the dragon,
lost the battle.

She picked up the pieces,
Phoenix from ashes.
They bat their eyelashes;
how dare she find peace.
Had this life not been,
enough of a thief?
Even the demons,
breathed
a sigh of relief.

Death consumes,
my existence.
Black widow,
close the window.
Lock the souls,
inside.
What's it going to take?
Just survive.
Tired skull,
crying eyes.
Female Grim Reaper,
I am your keeper.
Push the pain deeper,
flowers for your eyes.
Just stay alive.

I sleep curled
in the corner
every night.
A bed colored,
deep ocean blue.
Ours.
Just us two.
It's hard to leave here.
I pull the blinds tight.
It never gets dark enough.
The light always pours in.
I close my eyes,
imagine your steady breathing.
Hands folded across your chest.
I'm a mess.
My eyes are never
not full of tears.
Replay all the memories,
the years.
Our love is stronger,
than your fears.
Unlock the door,
please let me back in.
I'm suffocating.
I've died within.
Let me back in.

You can feel it
when it leaves you.
The happiness.
It had been wrapped
around your bones,
sewn into your heart
crisscrossed in your veins.
It's got claws
deep in your flesh.
It's teeth sunken in.
Then all at once
it's ripped happiness from you,
From your gut
like a sucker punch.
A forced exhale,
a breath you so badly
want to hold in.
And once it's gone,
you immediately crave it.
You forget what it feels like.
How it tasted
like his skin in the summer.
How it glimmered
like bedroom eyes.
Fast and quiet.
Fleeting.
You'd do anything
to have it back.

Up in the twisted Salem tree,
my raven watches over me.
Eyes of gold,
feathers charcoaled,
thorned roses
he's plucked for me.
Iron fence guarded,
but with my raven
perched upon it,
he will guide my soul
to the sea.
For this,
is the gravestone promise
he has made to me.

Hell-o.
Seat me on the left side,
queen to the blazing throne.
Angel on your shoulder.
Darkest secrets,
dreadful woes.
Scent the velvet halls,
lavender falls.
Midnight hair,
down my spine.
Words hushed,
wrapped in vines.

Watch me paint my eyes,
in golden mirrors.
Lipstick black,
Tattered wings
on my back.
Bad girls
don't finish last.
Bloody your knuckles,
sweet honeysuckle.

You don't know heaven,
unless you struggle.
Tuck a lily
behind my ear,

perfume my wrists.
Death smells
so sweet, dear.
What's left
to fear here?
Devilish bliss.

Stardust,
light illuminates me.
Does the roundness
of my blushed cheeks show?
Built from happiness.
Hair cascading down my spine,
the bones you used to see
when sorrow eradicated me.
The color of
a midnight waterfall.
Hands that have touched
loss too closely.
Lips that know
the kiss of death,
that quietly sits still
on my shoulder.

She speaks of nothing,
but dusts my collarbone with teardrops.
I visit my mother,
once a week.
I sit in the grass,
tracing the dash
between the years
she was earthside.
For your entire life,

You just never think
she will ever die.
But here I sit
another year creeping in,
whispering to the wind.

When you're little, the dark is what is terrifying.
I was taught to fear it, escape it. The monsters are there.
When we grow older, we realize the monsters are in the
light of day, not dark of night. It's the man you thought
was a gentle lover, the sickness that stole your mother,
the pain you cause unwillingly to others. In the dark,
I've found solace. The black of the ocean. The deepest pit
of hell. The devil has kissed my lips softly and wished me
well. In the dark, I've found a hand to hold. The will for
my story to be told. Sweet seduction, a burning cold.

Porcelain skin,
color of milk.
Splash of freckles,
constellation
across my back.
Indented shoulder blade,
birthmarked.
An angel's kiss.
Proof of wings,
from a past
existence.
Thorned roses,
crystal crown.
Steady eyes,
darkest brown.
How do you
see me?
Tell me,
loud.

Jagged edges,
softened.
Sea glass resurrection.
My rock,
protection.
You've been my go-to,
to get through
years of this life.
Carefully you've removed,
thorns from my roses.
Blooming,
in synchrony with you.
Symphony anew.
Black and blue,
skin renewed.

Attached,
Umbilical.
Captivated,
eyes of jade.
Love,
made.
In the water,
we waded.
We waited.
Outrun
our ghosts.
Your heart,
my home,
the host.
Feed the love,
grow.

I am imperfection.
Rough diamond,
picked from
long-gone mining.
Fresh start,
silver lining.
Bound in blood,
not planed wood.
The only one,
whoever could
decipher my misunderstood.

A nightmare wakes you,
in a panic.
Stop taking this life,
for granted.
Grazing knuckles,
while you're walking.
Smiling
hearing their voice,
midnight talking.
How you've memorized them,
map it out with eyes closed.

What sparks their fire,
hitting a nerve
walking the wire.
You cannot tell me,
life is not meant to be this.
That long slow kiss,
a promise, a wish.
Remember all of this.
The shit
is worth
the bliss.

Do you ever sit
and study her?
Glass full of brandy,
mouth like fire,
heart on the sleeve.
Balanced,
walking the wire.
Where's your
favorite freckle,
dusted across her skin?
Brown eyes
with a green speckle.

Cupid's bow, dipped.
Strawberry lips,
trace the little top divot.
Sun-flavored kiss.
Midnight soul,
a raven's heart.
Created a life,
did her part.
A soft belly
and a scar
to prove it.

Reoccurring dreams,
nighttime blues.
An ache to fill,
this empty womb.
A love made,
just us two.
Evergreen eyes,
strawberry hair,
sprinkled like petals everywhere.
Knobby knees,
a fighter's heart.
Perfect,
from the start.
Named after,
witch city.
Irish pretty.
Shining moon.
The lack of you,
looms.
How I wish,
we'd bloom.

Perched upon
the sickle,
like a murder
of crows.
Tell me how
this crescent flows.
The tides, the breeze,
the hum of the trees.
Safe in the crater,
as time ticks later.
Constellations,
call her Luna
to the left of Scorpius.
Even the man on the moon,
makes a shooting star wish.

Sacred places,
twin flame spaces.
Light the path,
welcome me home.
I feel the echo,
inside my bones.
Takes me places,
the rest don't know.
The dark,
doesn't scare me
like it used to.

Riverbed dirt,
citrus-colored blooms of wild,
hiding in the quiet.
The sway of the trees,
dance over me.
The sun peeking through leaves,
One of my favorite things to see.
Do they recognize me?

I'm a jagged piece of puzzle,
rough around the edges.
Cuss with red lips,
black nail polish.
Armored heart,
to a fault.
My favorite places are the ones that haunt.
Planted,
under oak trees.
Romanticize with the weary.
Overlooking cities, in spots no one can see.
Kiss the quiet, I need near me.

Release death
from my bones.
Demons,
from my home.
Evil,
will bring you
to your knees.
Forced prayers,
desperation.
Swear a soul,
to damnation.
His eyes
would turn black.
Crack.
Flames,
the dragon.
The pain,
the maddening.
Eye to eye,
the devil himself.

PART TWO

In Bloom

Can you name them?
The moments,
instances,
where you feel alive again.
Lungs,
that felt buried.
Resurrection.
The purity of the breath
you inhale.
Redondo Beach.
Sunrays slice navy-hued water.
Cinnamon-salted air puts waves in my hair.
A toe tipped in, Pacific Ocean.
Sunset layer.

Eternally barefoot
stubborn as they come.
My soul is quiet,
self-controlled.
It was tortured,
tired,
turbulent.
Teardrops lived in my eyelashes.

Now. . .
reborn, thriving, untroubled.
The pieces you helped pull
from the rubble.
Our love is without limits.
Warm belly,
stable base.
Peace in place.

Smoke and embers,
a scent to remember.
Fallen like a leaf,
without a sound.
Summer and autumn,
now a distant memory.
I sometimes come here to think.
Close my eyes and see flashes,
as snow coats my eyelashes.
Dream of the warmth,
flame heat against my face.
This will always be,
our favorite place.
When hearts seem distant,
my mind overthinks
it grows full of fear.
I always wind up here.
Seated on this stone,
with the earth cold.
Waiting for my summer throne.

Find me in the shadows
quietly, I will wait.
For my soul
will meet your body,
unwavering fate.
Lay out your darkness,
my hands will christen the cracks.
My wings have blackened,
tattered on my back.
Love my imperfections:
messy hair, combat boots.
Our demons will dance,
plant their roots.

Cover my eyes,
dandelions.
I wished for this,
On the little whisps.
Stem after stem.
Four-leaf clover,
pull me closer.
Lucky pennies,
in a dish.
Kiss me,
slowly.
Soul's glow,
eternally.

Wings.
Bat,
not angel.
Black,
darker than the night.
Wondrous moon,
tattoo.
Full of you.
Middle of my top lip,
your favorite kiss.
Only one,
who ever noticed this.
You know,
what makes me tick.
My heart,
this is it.

⌒⟶

Mental snapshots are my favorite thing. Moments too good for a photograph to capture, for they wouldn't do it justice. You on a Sunday October morning, gazing out the window at the leaves in full peak, like a fire in the sky so blue it hurts your eyes after a night spent tangled in crisp hotel sheets. I only sleep well when you're lost in dreams next to me. Where I can fall asleep in the nook you swear wasn't carved into your bones for me. On the skin I've grazed millions of times with my fingertips to put myself to sleep because you are home to me. You in a backward hat driving a pickup truck in the dead of summer with one hand on my knee and country music on the radio with fishing poles sliding around in its bed. Mosquito-bitten ankles and flushed cheeks because we couldn't resist each other while hidden under the canopy of trees so green. A cup of water in the holder full of wildflowers picked for me.

Hang your wings up, darlin'
show me your horns.
You cannot truly
love someone
until you see
where their heart
has thorns.

Your name carved in the bed-post carved in my bones.
Your light is inked on my finger, your heart is home.
The quiet of a morning stir.
The gravitational pull.
Not a word, just movements.
Morning sighs as the sun peeks through the cracks
of the heavy curtains.
Construction in the distance as summer gave a final
kiss on coastal lips,
a stone's throw away from anchored ships on a
seashell path
forever wrecked by the sea's wrath.
A lighthouse adorned atop of it.
The wind gusting, but me holding on.
Trying to stop it like I can control the weather.
It scares me every time when your toes touch the edge,
but you love the thrill of it.
Laugh as I pull you in.
"This always makes you nervous."

She looks best
in moon light
reflecting off her pale skin,
at midnight.
Drive her to the middle of nowhere.
The smell of early autumn
nestled in her hair.
Honey eyes,
take a dip.
Like the crescent,
of her hips.
Trace the bow
of her lips,
entwined fingertips.

I won't
wake you at dawn,
just promise me sunsets.
Moon eyed,
last of the fireflies.
Graveyard of stars,
safe in your arms.
Armed.
Apple-scented air, gun-smoke hair.
Seated on the wrap-around,
watch the sun sink down.
Sweet cider on my lips,
tastes better in a kiss.

Those mornings on the cusp of a season change, when you smell that sweet familiar scent in the air, but you can never name it. You've known it your whole life. You recognize it immediately on a stolen moment of a breeze. You can always pinpoint it to certain memories, like flipping through worn pages. The bittersweet end of summer, opening the door for flame-colored leaves. I'm a harvest baby; I yearn for the chill in my bones. The feel of the dirt cooling stone thrones. Ready for slumber. Autumn's gentle kiss on flushed lips.

Bury yourself within,
above the buried.
Thumb across my cheek,
to your squeeze around my neck.
Shallow breathing,
fill my mouth sticky sweet.
Sweat gleaming
hearts beating
synchrony.
Those fingers all over,
wish on me four-leaf clover.
I want dirty knees
and fists full of your skin.
Surrounding you,
pulling in.
Open me up slowly
flicking every page corner
like a book you've been dying to read.
Not just a want,
a need.
Throw my head back quiet scream,
fill me up deeply
drown in me.
Repeat.

I think we loved here, too. In a past life, me and you.
Cobblestone streets beneath our feet, the crunch of the
gravel to the path of the light to lead the lost home.
A stolen kiss. Every time I see it, I love you more.
Lay with me here, under the crow's nest of twisted
trees. Bury me deep in the dirt they once called wicked.
Next to the faded stones, "As above, so below."
Give me a silent street. Candlelight. A dark night.
A painted black house, that is quiet as a mouse.
The walls, velvet like the snake. Roses. Fossils in a vase.
This is our place. My hands, your face. Vow myself to
you at the feet of the beast. Whisper, hallelujah.

Into the wind I'm swallowed,
the hills of Gallows.
Let it carry me to the wharf.
Pass the gravel,
pass the shells
the ships swell.

My heart fell.
It balances on one of the five points.
The lighthouse, my wishing well.
Rising moon, catch me.
Drink me in
your light.

Trace the lifeline,
across my palm.
Your touch is fire—
ignite me.
Heartbeats,
synch.
Wine-red cheeks,
drink
me
in.
Your voice,
my worship hymns.
Indulge,
electric skin.

Controlled chaos.
Let's get lost,
in each other.
Your skin,
soft as butter.
There will never be another.
Don't need my eyes,
I've memorized.
You.
Mesmerize,
me.

In the still of the night, I quietly lay by your side and watch you sleep. Your steady breath, peace. Bare, inked bodies against the smoke-colored sheets. Lay my hand upon your armor chest, to feel your heartbeat.
The air is scented with the fresh soap on your skin.
I want to remember every moment, take all of you in.
Limbs wrapped, candlelight glow. Devour me, never let go. You're all I ever want to know.

Carve my name,
into the climbing tree.
Grown old with me,
under its leaves.
Branches wrap
like sturdy arms,
to keep me warm
from the snow.
Where you go, I go.
Isn't it funny,
how you just know?
I can hear your whispers,
through the dying firefly glow.
I just want you to know,
I love you so.

Every kiss
feels like the first time.
I always think
about that night.
Serendipity.
You cupped my face,
like I was fragile glass.
Studied me,
lash to lash.
Moving slowly,
made to last.
Crescent moon,
me and you.
Just like the universe
planned us two.
Lips brushed,
your touch
blood rush.
The trust.
It will always be us.

Mind wanderer,
self-proclaimed astronomer.
Study your eyes,
lost in the sky.
This world tries so hard to pull love apart.
Hold on, to my heart.
I don't need
an adorned finger.
I need our love,
to linger.
No proclaimed paper.
I can speak my truth to you, under the spring moon.
Tell me what you need me to do.
It's you, my love.
It will always be you.

Promise me love,
infinitely.
When moments are fleeting,
pumping hearts beating.
How the air smells,
a love spell.
The way your mouth tastes,
sweet cream and sugar.
How you put your hand,
draped across my waist.
Brush the wind-blown hair from my face.
My eyes, race.
Study you.
Embrace,
black lace.

Raven perched
in your twisted tree,
sing to me.
Tell me stories,
of meant to be.
Make a crown,
to adorn my hair.
Promise me,
you won't go anywhere.
Love so hard,
heart bursting in air.
Tuck your midnight feather, behind my ear.
Remind our souls why we are here.
For a love like this,
endless bliss.
Serendipitous.

Peace,
a nightmare-less sleep.
Restorative beats,
rumble the walls.
Feet,
no longer tiptoe
down the hall.
You're the constant,
through it all.
Weight of the world,
split for two.
Mind made up;
I choose you.

You sleep best,
in the pitch black.
Your hand rests on,
the small of my back.
Crack the window,
let the rain inside.
Stripped down,
nothing to hide.
Tell me all your secrets;
confide
in
me.

Drunk on you.
Honey on your lips.
Lick it off.
Pull me in for
another kiss.
Eat my heart,
suck the poison out.
Bury your roots inside me;
entwine them with my veins;
put your mouth to my ear;
whisper my name.
I'll praise
your devilish hymns,
worship glistening grin.
Heavenly sin,
drench my skin.
Breathe in.

The beads of sweat,
that glimmer
down the crease
of my crescent hip
that meet my thighs
tangled around you,
salt on my lips.
Midnight moon bliss.
We breathe.
In,
out.
Drink me in.
Slow down,
I can't get enough of you.

Inhale me.
Nothing else matters.
I can feel every inch of your soul
blending
with mine.
Wrap my legs
tighter
around you
like vines
ever thine.

Lunar eclipse,
midnight bliss.
Intoxicated,
your kiss.
Lips, hips, fingertips.
The magic of this.
Twinkly lights,
illuminate our nights.
Wear the moon,
nothing else.
Inhale me.
The apple,
flesh.

Weave the web
burn me at the stake.
I'll take my fate.
The crows are cawing
to take me home
to the sweetest love
I've ever known.
Run your hands
Down the curve
of the crescent moon.
Sharp like the knife
you keep in your pocket,
shining bright into our room.
Peace
in this tomb.

Blushed cheeks
wrinkled sheets.
Bodies flushed
the rush.
Your strong hands
to my hips.
Trace up
to my naked lips.
Entwine with my fingertips.

The back of my knuckles
dance
across the ocean
of these sheets.
You touch me
the softest.
Like feathers
dancing
across my skin.
My favorite sin.

⌒

I am wrinkled satin
you've smoothed
with your sturdy hands.
Hands that have held me together
through it all.
Death.
Life.
Love— a new beginning.
We've built it all our own.

Brick
by
brick.
The skeleton of every foundation,
the bones of a structure.
The bricks you placed
to the door of my home
to now lie beside me
in a bed all our own.
The color of the darkest storm.

My soul is steady within your heart,
I've placed it there for safe keeping.
There was a time when I couldn't keep anything
still.
My mind,
my body.
Your love has blanketed me like thunder-snow;
Lush, silent, patient.

Kiss me
in the elevator.
Green velvet walls
shining halls.
Bodies curled
reflected
in shining brass.
Promise me
it's not the last.

Grave reflections,
buried my imperfections.
Stripped down,
uninhibited.
Cover me,
beautiful darkness.
Plant me here,
in the fresh earth.
Dig my nails
in summer dirt.
A woman's worth.
I could rest here,
for a while.

Cradle my neck,
embrace my wild.
Sing to you,
I promise to.
Haunted melodies,
blissful chemistry.
Tonight's dream?
Take off my shoes,
stand on your feet to dance with you.
Two twirls and a dip will do.
Watching me,
watching you.

Circle of trust.
It will always be us.
Vowed in the cinder,
long after winter.
We have gathered
around these flames
from the first cricket chirp,
to the first sight of snow.
We were found here; saved,
survived here.
Our names carved in the limbs,
lifelong promises.
Dug ourselves deep
in the ash-covered dirt here.
This spot is magic,
nothing can scorch it.

Place a flower
everywhere it hurt.
Bury the first
deep in the dirt.
Two in the cracked cage
that covers my heart.
Blood-red petals for my eyes,
for the things
that still haunt.
Four for the pillow
that never saw sleep.
Five for the years
I won't keep.
Six for the loving hands
that now bring me
everlasting peace.

Drink up the sea,
You and me.
Your heart,
is home to me.
Tears on my cheeks,
salt you've tasted.
Patience,
the waiting.
Building,
our foundation.
Time,
no longer wasted.

I can smell,
the notes in your cologne.
Face in your neck,
honey, I'm home.
Do your demons
want to dance
with mine?
Lay me down,
in the pine.
Pitch black paths,
Two hands
intertwined.
Let's live among the trees.
Freckled shoulders,
butterfly leaves.
Your love,
fills me.

I want you,
unfiltered.
Rough cut diamond,
carved from the earth.
I want the mud,
I want the dirt
soaked under my fingernails.
Soul seeping,
into my blood stream.
No sight,
left unseen.
You've always told me,
"I'll be whatever you need."
Everlasting dream.

Garden of Eden.
You've given me a reason,
to want to live
every season of life
with you.
Eat the apple,
remove the shrapnel.
The past wreckage
has lost,
damage undone
we've won.
Tree of wisdom
lost souls,
forgiven.
Tree of life,
spending mine with you.
Under our crescent moon.

Float with me,
in the dark sea.
Drape my face,
with lush black lace.
Hair above me dancing,
oceanic crown.
Reign with me,
master of the deep.
See nothing,
but the whites of my eyes.
Fear won't paralyze;
it's our time.

Clover eyes,
never lie.
Memorize me.
Calloused hands,
a fighting man.
Hold me,
your once-lost treasure.
High stepping,
tall, wheat-colored grass.
Collapsed barns,
canopy of evergreens.
Hidden brooks,
serene green,
in your arms.
Hills of country, wild Virginia.
I'd go anywhere,
with you.

Meet me in our sanctuary,
cathedral forbidden forest.
Taste the sap, on my tongue.
Let your sticky fingers,
linger.
Trace my spine.
Wrap my heart,
vines.
Windy paths,
summer rain bath.
Run through the darkness,
your hand in mine.
Blinded by night,
guided by moonlight.

Guided,
the light of the moon.
Baptism,
the riverbed
and you.
Shadow of the trees, illuminate me.
You know
the darkest corners,
the doubts,
the broken,
my bricks and mortar.
Stacked them, triumphantly.
Words ring
the frogs sing,
"You are it.
Enough for me."

Take the time to bask in the
sanctity.
The moments,
you want to say it all.
A wharf town, planked dock
July heat,
late night breeze.
A little white home,
dimly lit door,
reflection on the water
you've been here before.
I've dreamt of this,
Deja vu.
You
love
me
too.

Together,
we bloom.
Where there is me,
there is you.
Sheets wrangle,
Legs tangled.
Irish eyes,
trace thighs.
Exhale,
sighs.
I don't believe
in false gods,
but your touch immerses me.
Holy water,
brand new.

The urgency
in touch.
A reminder,
we can't get enough.
One body,
connected.
Your mouth,
honeycomb sweet.
Moth to a flame,
whisper my name.
Hot heat,
like fire
wrapped within me.
Steady breathing,
moments fleeting.
Hearts beating,
synchrony.

When your heart
is quiet
and your mind
is loud,
let me love you
silently.
Head to chest we will rest;
this will always feel like home.
Wake up to you,
a skyline view
pink morning light
dusting the sky.
You don't know I'm watching,
but I always do.

⌒

Running on fumes
anxiety looms around every corner.
But then,
there was you.
Remember it all.
Every kiss at a red light,
the makeup after our first fight.
The blurted I love you.
Pillow talk,
until golden morning light.
Bed of the truck,
starry sky summer nights.
It's all right.
It's alright.

⌣⟋

Kindred,
in pace.
Step for step.
Quiet,
hearts race.
Sticks crack
underfoot.
Wandering our forest,
looking at you.
Sun rays creep,
retired winter dew.
I could stay here forever,
let the summer blaze through.
Watch the buds bloom.
Scatters of
yellow, purple, blue.
Start fresh,
brand new.

I get lost
in a mindset,
trapped
within it.
Buried,
above ground.
Dreaming,
of infinite.
Grasp tightly,
fists full
of clovers.
Make a wish.
Sunday drives,
all of this.

One day
when our bones are too tired to do all the things we've done,
we will sit hand in hand admiring the love we have
built from the ground up.
California sunsets
engulfed us
like fire in the sky.
Painted the canyons
golden glow on your skin.
Crescent moon perfection
all I saw was you.

I love you deeper
than the darkness of the woods.
In the quiet end of summer
a symphony of crickets.
Firefly paths
illuminating
like moon dust.

You love me stronger than the blue of the mountains
off the curved dirt back roads from the log house
on the hill.
My heart beats the loudest
in the still quiet dusk
of a buffalo sunset.

Quiet, makes my mind race.

I notice myself, in an abandoned place.

My heart hides, twisted in vine, secluded in the pines.

The ones that take a far drive,

but damn do they make you feel alive.

My soul is painted, in the burnt orange sunsets.

The ones with the pink peeking through the black
of the night hidden behind barns.

Early summer dew.

Nights that go by too soon.

Lyrics that carry you through.

We can leave the windows open
let the rain
come pouring inside.
You can park this truck
in a hurry.
We can watch it storm outside.
I'll trace the drops,
make my heart stop.
Inhale the cold.
Put my head in your neck.
Lay out the deck,
king and queen.
Crown full of black-eyed,
crescent moon tattoos.
Me and you.

I'll take a dusty dirt back road
with you in the country,
no one on the road but us.
You'll go anywhere I go
as long as you get to steal a kiss on the drive.
I've never felt so alive.
Moonlit riverbed;
wildflower path.
Baptize me
in your clover eyes,
mesmerize.
This love is my new religion.

Wildflower.
How he has mended you
a tattered heart, brand new.
Sewn together with fishing line.
His skin smells of pine.
Hands that he calls mine.
A heart to call my own,
a soul,
home.

Make a home
among the leaves.
X marks the spot,
between a fork
in the trees.
Daytime sun gleams.
Night fall raindrops,
soak the canopy.
Shelter in
familiar dew.
Summer crystals,
cover you.
Dusk melody,
Moon beams
lush trees.
Firefly,
dream of thee.
This is where I will be.

I love dusk to moonlight,
when the light hits
just right.
Pure silence,
heat still radiating
into the night.
I live for that late-July summer glow,
when the sun dips below
the line of indigo clouds kissing the ground.

Where were you,
when you felt found?
Manifestations,
all around.
Close your eyes
rest your bones
in the blades of grass.
Yearn.
Dig your bare heels
into the dirt.
Heaven on earth.

Dip your fingers in my ocean,
I want your skin
under my nails.
The rush overflowing,
like waves crash the sand.
Pull my leg closer,
to dive deeper.
Sweat at the nape of my neck.
Your spit like honey,
pools in my mouth.
Suck your finger,
swallow it down.
Graze your teeth
along each curve.
Hands on the wheel,
make you swerve
electrified nerves.
Fingertips slowly dip into me,
taste my cherry sweet.
Flip me over,
repeat.

Cleanse me,
in your sea.
Salted skin,
embraces me.
Naked poetry.

One day we're going to build us a home from scratch
with all the pennies we saved. Set back far in the
thick of the woods with a porch that wraps around
the bones of the house that kisses the mud of a river.
You'll promise me we will build a room for all the books
I will write you, with floor to ceiling built-in shelves for
all my precious words. They'll hang off your lips. In the
middle of fall, you'll wake in the morning and cover me
with our quilt quietly not to wake me, but the moment
I feel you unwrap yourself from me, I stir, asking for
five more minutes. The walls will echo with the quiet
love we poured ourselves into both battered and still
healing. Scarred love is the purest form. It's been
touched, burned, and beaten, but its flame will never
ash. Ash like the color of the ceilings I'll beg you to
paint, because it reminds me of the summer night sky.
Chasing constellations. The comfort of silence.

Down on the riverbed,
hush of dusk in the sky.
Bed of the truck,
firework eyes.
July weekends,
tucked away in the trees.
We can see them,
but to them, we're a mystery.
Rush of the water,
cricket orchestra.
Sanctuary.
Twinkling fireflies,
as far as I can see.
Tell me,
how long
have you,
loved me?

Hot heat,
inferno.
Hair,
red as flames.
Tell me you love me.
I dance barefoot
in the soot.
Sparks of fire,
a veil of flowers
engulf my head.
Lay me down,
in a wildflower bed.
I want to know your secrets,
your haunts, fears.
Only I can hear,
over the roar of the blaze.
This fire
will never
burn out.

⌣⟶

Highest point,
we overlook the city.
Fire sunset soaks the sky.
Glowing cross illuminates the night.
Sacred spots,
we have planted.
Roots entwined,
the trees you've climbed.
Wrap my arms around you,
branches.
I love to watch you stare.
Put yellow flowers,
in my hair.
You've picked them,
wild.

Clouds rolled through,
as water rushed past.
Find a spot in the woods,
wait while the rain passed.
Canopy of trees.
One rock shared,
for you and me.
Not a single drop,
touched us.
Burrowed tight,
under the leaves.
Two fishing poles, at our feet.
Your scent,
everlasting.
Pine,
my sweet.

Follow me
down all the paths
we make unknown.
Winding trails
in the heat of the summer,
rushing water
the buzz of the lines
through the vines.

I always ask you,
did you ever think
you'd be mine?
We fought for this life.
I want to drown in you
like the Pacific in August.
You make me feel
electrically alive.

I've seen the facets in the labyrinth of your alluring mind.

Live energy weaving through electric cerulean vines.

I know the pathways through the lush forest of
your evergreen gaze.

I'll take any serendipity to look deeper.

Darker.

When the sky is the brightest, we've ever seen it,
illuminated by a wolf moon.

We were the only ones existing, just me and you.

There is no peace in solitude,

but there is when I've melted into you.

The house is full of flowers you bring me
on a Monday afternoon,
ever blooming, ever changing.
My heart rests in peace.
All the things I once wished for
are now tangled in these sheets.
I used to dream of the day you'd whisper,
"You're forever mine."
Now we fall asleep
with fingers and bodies intertwined
lips down necks,
breathless morning sighs.
There were seasons I begged love to stay,
left rooms where silence had more to say.
But you,
you stayed.
Now the coffee steams between us;
your laugh floats through the kitchen like light.
The sheets smell like lavender and you.
Soft things I treasure to hold.
This isn't just love.
It's everything that grew after the storm.
And somehow,
you are still here.
Hands full of flowers.

⌣⟶

Blooming,
In synchrony with you.

AUTHOR BIO

KELLIE KAMINSKAS is a passionate storyteller hailing from the beautiful state of Connecticut. From earning her BA with a focus in Creative Writing and English Literature from UMass Amherst UWW, Kellie has honed her skills in crafting captivating tales that transport readers to new or familiar worlds. She draws inspiration from the joys and challenges of her lived experiences. Kellie is not only a two-time award-winning author but also an engaging speaker, available for virtual or in-person visits to libraries and events. (Kelliekaminskas.com)

LET'S STAY CONNECTED

Website: www.kelliekaminskas.com

Instagram: @kellie.kaminskas